Around the World

Food

Margaret C. Hall

Heinemann Library
Chicago, Illinois

© 2001 Reed Educational & Professional Publishing
Published by Heinemann Library,
an imprint of Reed Educational & Professional Publishing,
Chicago, IL 60602

Customer Service 888-454-2279

Visit our website at www.heinemannlibrary.com

Designed by Lisa Buckley
Printed in Hong Kong

05 04 03 02 01
10 9 8 7 6 5 4 3 2

Library of Congress Cataloging-in-Publication Data
Hall, Margaret, 1947–
    Food / Margaret C. Hall.
        p. cm.--(Around the world)
    Includes bibliographical references and index.
    ISBN 1-58810-102-9 (library binding)
    1. Gastronomy--Juvenile literature. I. Title. II. Around the world (Chicago, Ill.)

TX641.H34 2001
641.3--dc21

                                        00-063268

Acknowledgments
The author and publishers are grateful to the following for permission to reproduce copyright material:
Robert Frerck/Tony Stone, p., 1, 11; Wolfgang Kaehler, pp.4a, 17, 21; Keren Su/Tony Stone, p., 4b; Sharon Smith/Bruce Coleman, Inc., p. 4c; Anna E. Zuckermann/Photo Edit, p. 5; Fulvio Eccardi/ECCAR/Bruce Coleman, Inc., p. 6; Wayne Estep/Tony Stone, p. 7; David Hiser/Tony Stone, p. 8; James Nelson/Tony Stone, p. 9; Bob Krist/Corbis, p. 10; Mike Price/Bruce Coleman, Inc., p. 12; Penny Tweedie/Corbis, p. 13; Paul Conklin/Photo Edit, p. 14; Bios (Klein & Hubert)/Peter Arnold, p. 15; Scott Camazine/Photo Researchers, p. 16; Galen Rowell/Corbis, p. 18; Art Wolfe/Tony Stone, p. 19; Jeff Greenberg/Photo Edit, p. 20; Bryan Mullennix/MULLE/Bruce Coleman, Inc., p. 22; Jeff Greenbert/Peter Arnold, p. 23; Holt Studios/Photo Researcher, p. 24; Carl Purcell/Photo Researchers, p. 25; Tom Stewart/The Stock Market, p. 26; Richard Hutchings/Photo Researchers, p. 27; Ric Ergenbright, p. 28; Tony Freeman/Photo Edit, p. 29.

Cover: Fulvio Eccardi/ECCAR/Bruce Coleman, Inc.

Every effort has been made to contact copyright holders of any material reproduced in this book. Any omissions will be rectified in subsequent printings if notice is given to the publisher.

Some words are shown in bold, **like this.** You can find out what they mean by looking in the glossary.

Contents

People Have Needs

People everywhere have the same **needs.**
They need food, clothing, water, and
homes. They also need to be able to get
from place to place.

Where people live makes a difference in what they eat and wear. It makes a difference in their homes and the kinds of **transportation** they use.

People Need Food

No one can live without food. Food gives people **energy** and makes their bodies grow. Eating the right kinds of food keeps people healthy.

There are other reasons for eating, too. People share food to show that they are friends. They eat together to **celebrate** special days.

Getting Food

What people eat depends on the **climate** where they live. It also depends on the **resources** they have nearby.

Some people grow, gather, or hunt their own food. Other people get all the food they eat from stores or markets.

Food Around the World

Food **customs** in one place may seem strange in another. Some people think termites and other insects are a treat. Others might eat raw fish.

Even a food that everyone eats is not always the same. Bread in one part of the world might not look or taste like the bread in another part!

Growing Food

People grow many kinds of **crops** that are used for food. **Grains** like rice, wheat, corn, and barley feed people all around the world.

People also grow fruits and vegetables to eat. The kinds of fruits and vegetables they grow depend on the **climate** where they live.

Finding Food

In some places, people do not buy much food. They get most of their food from the land around them.

People grow some of the food they eat. They also pick wild foods such as berries and mushrooms. They hunt animals and catch fish to eat.

Raising Animals for Food

People also **raise** animals that are used for food. Some people keep animals for the milk or eggs they give.

Other animals are raised for their meat. Many people eat the meat of animals like cows, pigs, sheep, and chickens.

Food from the Water

Oceans, lakes, and rivers are home to many fish and other animals. People who live near water eat a lot of these foods. They also eat water plants, such as seaweed.

The kind of **seafood** people eat also depends on where they live. Some fish are caught in warm water. Other fish, like salmon and whitefish, live in cooler water.

Food in Tropical Places

Tropical places are hot and wet. Many fruits and vegetables grow well in tropical **climates.** Fruits like bananas, pineapples, and mangoes grow only in tropical places.

Tropical climates are also good for **crops** that need lots of water, such as rice. Many fish live in tropical waters, too.

Food in Temperate Places

Temperate climates are warm in summer and cold in winter. **Grains** such as wheat and barley grow well in these places. So do fruits and vegetables such as apples and peas.

During the winter, **crops** cannot be grown outside in temperate climates. People must buy food or use foods they have saved for the cold weather.

Food in Cold Places

In a cold **climate,** the **growing season** is very short. Many plant foods can only be grown in **greenhouses.** This means they cost more to buy.

Root vegetables, such as potatoes and carrots, have short growing seasons. They keep for a long time, too. People eat these vegetables along with fish and meat.

Special Food

People eat special foods as part of **festivals** or when they **celebrate** a special day. In some places, people roast a whole pig or goat. In other places, there might be special desserts.

Many people eat foods that show their **religious beliefs.** They may eat a special bread or a meal of vegetables. Some people never eat certain foods because of what they believe.

Food on the Move

Food is sent from where it is grown and sold to people far away. It is moved in trucks, trains, ships, and airplanes.

Large **supermarkets** sell foods from all over the world. A fruit grown in a **tropical** country might be eaten by someone who lives in a cold **climate**.

Amazing Food Facts

✪ In China, some people eat earthworm soup when they are sick.

✪ Some foods can be deadly! The puffer fish is a treat in Japan. However, if it is not fixed in the right way, it is poisonous.

✪ Bird's-nest soup is made from the nests of one kind of bird. People climb high, rocky cliffs to collect the nests. They sell them for a lot of money.

✪ Does seaweed ice cream sound good? Believe it or not, some ice cream has a kind of seaweed in it!

✪ People have been eating pancakes longer than almost any other food. Pancakes are called different names in different places, such as tortillas, latkes, or crêpes.

Glossary

celebrate   to have a party for a special event or holiday

climate   year-to-year weather for an area

crop   plant grown for food

custom   way something has been done or made for a long time

energy   ability to move about and be active

festival   time of celebration, usually with special events

grain   plant that produces seeds or kernels used as food, such as rice, oats, wheat, or barley

greenhouse   building where plants can be grown in cold weather

growing season   time when the weather is warm enough for plants to grow

needs   things people must have in order to live

raise   to care for an animal or plant until it is fully grown

religious belief   what a person believes about God

resource   item available for use

root vegetable   plant with roots that are eaten, such as potatoes, carrots, turnips, or radishes

seafood   animals that live in water and can be eaten, such as fish, clams, or crabs

supermarket   large food market

temperate   place with warm summers and cool or cold winters

transportation   ways people move from place to place

tropical   place where the weather is hot and rainy

More Books to Read

Bryant-Mole, Karen. *Food*. Chicago: Heinemann Library, 1999.

Burton, Margie, Cathy French, and Tammy James. *Food Around the World*. Pelham, N.Y.: Benchmark Education Company, 1999.

Lakin, Patricia. *Food Around the World*. Woodbridge, Conn.: Blackbirch Press, 1999. An older reader can help you with this book.

Index